MADAME DE

by

Elbert Hubbard

Far from gaining assurance in meeting Bonaparte oftener, he intimidated me daily more and more. I confusedly felt that no emotion of the heart could possibly take effect upon him. He looks upon a human being as a fact or as a thing, but not as a fellow-creature. He does not hate any more than he loves; there is nothing for him but himself; all other things are so many ciphers. The force of his will lies in the imperturbable calculation of his selfishness.
—*Reflections*

Fate was very kind to Madame De Stael.

She ran the gamut of life from highest love to direst pain—from rosy dawn to blackest night. Name if you can another woman who touched life at so many points! Home, health, wealth, strength, honors, affection, applause, motherhood, loss, danger, death, defeat, sacrifice, humiliation, illness, banishment, imprisonment, escape. Again comes hope—returning strength, wealth, recognition, fame tempered by opposition, home, a few friends, and kindly death—cool, all-enfolding death.

If Harriet Martineau showed poor judgment in choosing her parents, we can lay no such charge to the account of Madame De Stael.

They called her "The Daughter of Necker," and all through life she delighted in the title. The courtier who addressed her thus received a sunny smile and a gentle love-tap on his cheek for pay. A splendid woman is usually the daughter of her father, just as strong men have noble mothers.

Jacques Necker was born in Geneva, and went up to the city, like many another country boy, to make his fortune. He carried with him to Paris innocence, health, high hope, and twenty francs in silver. He found a place as porter or "trotter" in a bank. Soon they made him clerk.

A letter came one day from a correspondent asking for a large loan, and setting forth a complex financial scheme in which the bank was invited to join. M. Vernet, the head of the establishment, was away, and young Necker took the matter in hand. He made a detailed statement of the scheme, computed probable losses, weighed the pros and cons, and when the employer returned, the plan, all worked out, was on his desk, with young Necker's advice that the loan be made.

"You seem to know all about banking!" was the sarcastic remark of M. Vernet.

"I do," was the proud answer.

"You know too much; I'll just put you back as porter."

The Genevese accepted the reduction and went back as porter without repining. A man of small sense would have resigned his situation at once, just as men are ever forsaking Fortune when she is about to smile; witness Cato committing suicide on the very eve of success.

There is always a demand for efficient men; the market is never glutted; the cities are hungry for them—but the trouble is, few men are efficient.

"It was none of his business!" said M. Vernet to his partner, trying to ease conscience with reasons.

"Yes; but see how he accepted the inevitable!"

"Ah! true, he has two qualities that are the property only of strong men: confidence and resignation. I think—I think I was hasty!"

So young Necker was reinstated, and in six months was cashier, in three years a partner.

Not long after, he married Susanna Curchod, a poor governess.

But Mademoiselle Curchod was rich in mental endowment: refined, gentle, spiritual, she was a true mate to the high-minded Necker. She was a Swiss, too, and if you know how a young man and a young woman, countryborn, in a strange city are attracted to each other, you will better understand this particular situation.

Some years before, Gibbon had loved and courted the beautiful Mademoiselle Curchod in her quiet home in the Jura Mountains. They became engaged. Gibbon wrote home, breaking the happy news to his parents.

"Has the beautiful Curchod of whom you sing, a large dowry?" inquired the mother.

"She has no dowry! I can not tell a lie," was the meek answer. The mother came on and extinguished the match in short order.

Gibbon never married. But he frankly tells us all about his love for Susanna Curchod, and relates how he visited her, in her splendid Paris home. "She greeted me without embarrassment," says Gibbon, resentfully; "and in the evening Necker left us together in the parlor, bade me good-night, and lighting a candle went off to bed!"

Gibbon, historian and philosopher, was made of common clay (for authors are made of clay, like plain mortals), and he could not quite forgive Madame Necker for not being embarrassed on meeting her former lover, neither could he forgive Necker for not being jealous.

But that only daughter of the Neckers, Germaine, pleased Gibbon—pleased him better than the mother, and Gibbon extended his stay in Paris and called often.

"She was a splendid creature," Gibbon relates; "only seventeen, but a woman grown, physically and mentally; not handsome, but dazzling, brilliant, emotional, sensitive, daring!"

Gibbon was a bit of a romanticist, as all historians are, and he no doubt thought it would be a fine denouement to life's play to capture the daughter of his old sweetheart, and avenge himself on Fate and the unembarrassed Madame Necker and the unpiqued husband, all at one fell stroke—and she would not be dowerless either. Ha, ha!

But Gibbon forgot that he was past forty, short in stature, and short of breath, and "miles around," as Talleyrand put it.

"I quite like you," said the daring daughter, as the eloquent Gibbon sat by her side at a dinner.

"Why shouldn't you like me—I came near being your papa!"

"I know, and would I have looked like you?"

"Perhaps."

"What a calamity!"

Even then she possessed that same bubbling wit that was hers years later when she sat at table with D'Alembert. On one side of the great author was Madame Recamier, famous for beauty (and later for a certain "Beauty-Cream"), on the other the daughter of Necker.

"How fortunate!" exclaimed D'Alembert with rapture; "how fortunate I sit between Wit and Beauty!"

"Yes, and without possessing either," said Wit.

No mistake, the girl's intellect was too speedy even for Gibbon. She fenced all 'round him and over him, and he soon discovered that she was icily gracious to every one, save her father alone. For him she seemed to outpour all the lavish love of her splendid womanhood. It was unlike the usual calm affection of father and daughter. It was a great and absorbing love, of which even the mother was jealous.

"I can't just exactly make 'em out," said Gibbon, and withdrew in good order.

Before Necker was forty he had accumulated a fortune, and retired from business to devote himself to literature and the polite arts.

"I have earned a rest," he said; "besides, I must have leisure to educate my daughter."

Men are constantly "retiring" from business, but someway the expected Elysium of leisure forever eludes us. Necker had written several good pamphlets and showed the world that he had ability outside of money-making. He was appointed Resident Minister of Geneva at the Court of France. Soon after he became President of the French East India Company, because there was no one else with mind broad enough to fill the place. His house was the gathering-place of many eminent scholars and statesmen. Necker was quiet and reserved; his wife coldly brilliant, cultured, dignified, religious. The daughter made good every deficiency in both.

She was tall, finely formed, but her features were rather heavy, and in repose there was a languor in her manner and a blankness in her face. This seeming dulness marks all great actors, but the heaviness is only on the surface; it often covers a sleeping volcano. On recognizing an acquaintance, Germaine Necker's face would be illumined, and her smile would light a room. She could pronounce a man's name so he would be ready to throw himself at her feet, or over a precipice for her. And she could listen in a way that complimented; and by a sigh, a nod, an exclamation, bring out the best—such thoughts as a man never knew he had. She made people surprise themselves with their own genius; thus proving that to make a good impression means to make the man pleased with himself. "Any man can be brilliant with her," said a nettled competitor; "but if she wishes, she can sink all women in a room into creeping things."

She knew how to compliment without flattering; her cordiality warmed like wine, and her ready wit, repartee, and ability to thaw all social ice and lead conversationalong any line, were accomplishments which perhaps have never been equaled. The women who "entertain" often only depress; they are so glowing that everybody else feels himself punk. And these people who are too clever are very numerous; they seem inwardly to fear rivals, and are intent on working while it is called the day.

Over against these are the celebrities who sit in a corner and smile knowingly when they are expected to scintillate. And the individual who talks too much at one time is often painfully silent at another—as if he had made New-Year resolves. But the daughter of Necker entered into conversation with candor and abandon; she gave herself to others, and knew whether they wished to talk or to listen. On occasion, she could monopolize conversation until she seemed the only person in the room; but all talent was brighter for the added luster of her own. This simplicity, this utter frankness, this complete absence of self-consciousness, was like the flight of a bird that never doubts its power, simply because it never thinks of it. Yet continual power produces arrogance, and the soul unchecked finally believes in its own omniscience.

Of course such a matrimonial prize as the daughter of Necker was sought for, even fought for. But the women who can see clear through a man, like a Roentgen ray, do not invite soft demonstration. They give passion a chill. Love demands a little illusion; it must be clothed in mystery. And although we find evidences that many youths stood in the hallways and sighed, the daughter of Necker never saw fit by a nod to bring them to her feet. She was after bigger game—she desired the admiration and approbation of archbishops, cardinals, generals, statesmen, great authors.

Germaine Necker had no conception of what love is.

Many women never have. Had this fine young woman met a man with intellect as clear, mind as vivid, and heart as warm as her own, and had he pierced her through with a wit as strong and keen as she herself wielded, her pride would have been broken and she might have paused. Then they might have looked into each other's eyes and lost self there. And had she thus known love it would have been a complete passion, for the woman seemed capable of it.

A better pen than mine has written, "A woman's love is a dog's love." The dog that craves naught else but the presence of his master, who is faithful to the one and whines out his life on that master's grave, waiting for the caress that never comes and the cheery voice that is never heard—that's the way a woman loves! A woman may admire, respect, revere and obey, but she does not love until a passion seizes upon her that has in it the abandon of Niagara. Do you remember how Nancy Sikes crawls inch by inch to reach the hand of Bill, and reaching it, tenderly caresses the coarse fingers that a moment before clutched her throat, and dies content? That's the love of woman! The prophet spoke of something "passing the love of woman," but the prophet was wrong—there's nothing does.

So Germaine Necker, the gracious, the kindly, the charming, did not love. However, she married—married Baron De Stael, the Swedish Ambassador. He was thirty-seven, she was twenty. De Stael was good-looking, polite, educated. He always smiled at the right time, said bright things in the right way, kept silence when he should, and made no enemies because he agreed with everybody about everything. Stipulations were made; a long agreement was drawn up; it was signed by the party of the first and duly executed by the party of the second part; sealed, witnessed, sworn to, and the priest was summoned.

It was a happy marriage. The first three years of married life were the happiest Madame De Stael ever knew, she said long afterward.

Possibly there are hasty people who imagine they detect tincture of iron somewhere in these pages: these good people will say, "Gracious me! why not?"

And so I will at once admit that these respectable, well-arranged, and carefully planned marriages are often happy and peaceful.

The couple may "raise" a large family and slide through life and out of it without a splash. I will also admit that love does not necessarily imply happiness—more often 't is a pain, a wild yearning, and a vague unrest; a haunting sense of heart-hunger that drives a man into exile repeating abstractedly the name "Beatrice! Beatrice!" And so all the moral I will make now is simply this: the individual who has not known an all-absorbing love has not the spiritual vision that is a passport to Paradise. He forever yammers between the worlds, fit for neither Heaven nor Hell.

Necker retired from business that he might enjoy peace; his daughter married for the same reason. It was stipulated that she should never be separated from her father. She who stipulates is lost, so far as love goes—but no matter! Married women in France are greater lions in society than maidens can possibly hope to be. The marriage-certificate serves at once as a license for brilliancy, daring, splendor, and it is also a badge of respectability. The marriage-certificate is a document that in all countries is ever taken care of by the woman and never by the man.

And this document is especially useful in France, as French dames know. Frenchmen are afraid of an unmarried woman—she means danger, damages, a midnight marriage and other awful things. An unmarried woman in France can not hope to be a social leader; and to be a social leader was the one ambition of Madame De Stael.

It was called the salon of Madame De Stael now. Baron De Stael was known as the husband of Madame De Stael. The salon of Madame Necker was only a matter of reminiscence. The daughter of Necker was greater than her father, and as for Madame Necker, she was a mere figure in towering headdress, point lace and diamonds. Talleyrand summed up the case when he said, "She is one of those dear old things that have to be tolerated."

Madame De Stael had a taste for literature from early womanhood. She wrote beautiful little essays and read them aloud to her company, and her manuscripts had a circulation like unto her father's bank-notes. She had the faculty of absorbing beautiful thoughts and sentiments, and no woman ever expressed them in a more graceful way. People said she was the greatest woman author of her day. "You mean of all time," corrected Diderot. They called her "the High Priestess of Letters," "the Minerva of Poetry," "Sappho Returned," and all that. Her commendation meant success and her indifference failure. She knew politics, too, and her hands were on all wires. Did she wish to placate a minister, she invited him to call, and once there he was as putty in her hands. She skimmed the surface of all languages, all arts, all history, but best of all she knew the human heart.

Of course there was a realm of knowledge she wist not of—the initiates of which never ventured within her scope. She had nothing for them—they kept away. But the proud, the vain, the ambitious, the ennui-ridden, the people-who-wish-to-be, and who are ever looking for the strong man to give them help—these thronged her parlors.

And when you have named these you have named all those who are foremost in commerce, politics, art, education, philanthropy and religion. The world is run by second-rate people. The best are speedily crucified, or else never heard of until long after they are dead.

Madame De Stael, in Seventeen Hundred Eighty-eight, was queen of the people who ran the world—-at least the French part of it.

But intellectual power, like physical strength, endures but for a day. Giants who have a giant's strength and use it like a giant must be put down. If you have intellectual power, hide it!

Do thy daily work in thine own little way and be content. The personal touch repels as well as attracts. Thy presence is a menace—thy existence an affront—beware! They are weaving a net for thy feet, and hear you not the echo of hammering, as of men building a scaffold?

Go read history! Thinkest thou that all men are mortal save thee alone, and that what has befallen others can not happen to thee?

The Devil has no title to this property he now promises. Fool! thou hast no more claim on Fate than they who have gone before, and what has come to others in like conditions must come to thee. God himself can not stay it; it is so written in the stars. Power to lead men! Pray that thy prayer shall ne'er be granted—'t is to be carried to the topmost pinnacle of Fame's temple tower, and there cast headlong upon the stones beneath. Beware! beware!!

Madame De Stael was of an intensely religious nature throughout her entire life; such characters swing between license and asceticism. But the charge of atheism told largely against her even among the so-called liberals, for liberals are often very illiberal. Marie Antoinette gathered her skirts close about her and looked at the "Minerva of Letters" with suspicion in her big, open eyes; cabinet officers forgot her requests to call, and when a famous wit once coolly asked, "Who was that Madame De Stael we used to read about?" people roared with laughter.

Necker, as Minister of Finance, had saved the State from financial ruin; then had been deposed and banished; then recalled. In September, Seventeen Hundred Ninety, he was again compelled to flee. He escaped to Switzerland, disguised as a pedler. The daughter wished to accompany him, but this was impossible, for only a week before she had given birth to her first child.

But favor came back, and in the mad tumult of the times the freedom of wit and sparkle of her salon became a need to the poets and philosophers, if city wits can be so called.

Society shone as never before. In it was the good nature of the mob. It was no time to sit quietly at home and enjoy a book—men and women must "go somewhere," they must "do something." The women adopted the Greek costume and appeared in simple white robes caught at the shoulders with miniature stilettos. Many men wore crape on their arms in pretended memory of friends who had been kissed by Madame Guillotine. There was fever in the air, fever in the blood, and the passions held high carnival. In solitude, danger depresses all save the very strongest, but the mob (ever the symbol of weakness) is made up of women—it is an effeminate thing. It laughs hysterically at death and cries, "On with the dance!" Women represent the opposite poles of virtue.

The fever continues: a "poverty party" is given by Madame De Stael, where men dress in rags and women wear tattered gowns that ill conceal their charms. "We must get used to it," she said, and everybody laughed. Soon, men in the streets wear red nightcaps, women appear in nightgowns, rich men wear wooden shoes, and young men in gangs of twelve parade the avenues at night carrying heavy clubs, hurrahing for this or that.

Yes, society in Paris was never so gay.

The salons were crowded, and politics was the theme. When the discussion waxed too warm, some one would start a hymn and all would chime in until the contestants were drowned out and in token of submission joined in the chorus.

But Madame De Stael was very busy all these days. Her house was filled with refugees, and she ran here and there for passports and pardons, and beseeched ministersand archbishops for interference or assistance or amnesty or succor and all those things that great men can give or bestow or effect or filch. And when her smiles failed to win the wished-for signature, she still had tears that would move a heart of brass.

About this time Baron De Stael fades from our vision, leaving with Madame three children.

"It was never anything but a 'mariage de convenance' anyway, what of it ?" and Madame bursts into tears and throws herself into Farquar's arms.

"Compose yourself, my dear—you are spoiling my gown," says the Duchesse.

"I stood him as long as I could," continued Madame.

"You mean he stood you as long as he could."

"You naughty thing!—why don't you sympathize with me?"

Then both women fall into a laughing fit that is interrupted by the servant, who announces Benjamin Constant.

Constant came as near winning the love of Madame De Stael as any man ever did. He was politician, scholar, writer, orator, courtier. But with it all he was a boor, for when he had won the favor of Madame De Stael he wrote a long letter to Madame Charriere, with whom he had lived for several years in the greatest intimacy, giving reasons why he had forsaken her, and ending with an ecstacy in praise of the Stael.

If a man can do a thing more brutal than to humiliate one woman at the expense of another, I do not know it. And without entering any defense for the men who love several women at one time, I wish to make a clear distinction between the men who bully and brutalize women for their own gratification and the men who find their highest pleasure in pleasing women. The latter may not be a paragon, yet as his desire is to give pleasure, not to corral it, he is a totally different being from the man who deceives, badgers, humiliates, and quarrels with one who can not defend herself, in order that he may find an excuse for leaving her.

A good many of Constant's speeches were written by Madame De Stael, and when they traveled together through Germany he no doubt was a great help to her in preparing the "De l'Allemagne."

But there was a little man approaching from out the mist of obscurity who was to play an important part in the life of Madame De Stael. He had heard of her wide-reaching influence, and such an influence he could not afford to forego— it must be used to further his ends.

Yet the First Consul did not call on her, and she did not call on the First Consul. They played a waiting game, "If he wishes to see me, he knows that I am home Thursdays!" she said with a shrug.

"Yes, but a man in his position reverses the usual order: he does not make the first call!"

"Evidently!" said Madame, and the subject dropped with a dull thud.

Word came from somewhere that Baron De Stael was seriously ill. The wife was thrown into a tumult of emotion. She must go to him at once—a wife's duty was to her husband first of all. She left everything, and hastening to his bedside, there ministered to him tenderly. But death claimed him. The widow returned to Paris clothed in deep mourning. Crape was tied on the door-knocker and the salon was closed.

The First Consul sent condolences.

"The First Consul is a joker," said Dannion solemnly, and took snuff.

In six weeks the salon was again opened. Not long after, at a dinner, Napoleon and Madame De Stael sat side by side. "Your father was a great man," said Napoleon.

He had gotten in the first compliment when she had planned otherwise. She intended to march her charms in a phalanx upon him, but he would not have it so. Her wit fell flat and her prettiest smile brought only the remark, "If the wind veers north it may rain."

They were rivals—that was the trouble. France was not big enough for both.

Madame De Stael's book about Germany had been duly announced, puffed, printed. Ten thousand copies were issued and—seized upon by Napoleon's agents and burned.

"The edition is exhausted," cried Madame, as she smiled through her tears and searched for her pocket-handkerchief.

The trouble with the book was that nowhere in it was Napoleon mentioned. Had Napoleon never noticed the book, the author would have been woefully sorry. As it was she was pleased, and when the last guest had gone she and Benjamin Constant laughed, shook hands, and ordered lunch.

But it was not so funny when Fouche called, apologized, coughed, and said the air in Paris was bad.

So Madame De Stael had to go—it was "Ten Years of Exile." In that book you can read all about it. She retired to Coppet, and all the griefs, persecutions, disappointments and heartaches were doubtless softened by the inward thought of the distinction that was hers in being the first woman banished by Napoleon and of being the only woman he thoroughly feared.

When it came Napoleon's turn to go and the departure for Elba was at hand, it will be remembered he bade good-by personally to those who had served him so faithfully. It was an affecting scene when he kissed his generals and saluted the swarthy grenadiers in the same way. When told of it Madame picked a petal or two from her bouquet and said, "You see, my dears, the difference is this: while Judas kissed but one, the Little Man kissed forty."

Napoleon was scarcely out of France before Madame was back in Paris with all her books and wit and beauty. An ovation was given the daughter of Necker such as Paris alone can give.

But Napoleon did not stay at Elba, at least not according to any accounts I have read.

When word came that he was marching on Paris, Madame hastily packed up her manuscripts and started in hot haste for Coppet.

But when the eighty days had passed and the bugaboo was safely on board the "Bellerophon," she came back to the scenes she loved so well and to what for her was the only heaven—Paris.

She has been called a philosopher and a literary light. But she was only socio-literary. Her written philosophy does not represent the things she felt were true— simply those things she thought it would be nice to say. She cultivated literature, only that she might shine. Love, wealth, health, husband, children—all were sacrificed that she might lead society and win applause. No one ever feared solitude more: she must have those about her who would minister to her vanity and upon whom she could shower her wit. As a type her life is valuable, and in these pages that traverse the entire circle of feminine virtues and foibles she surely must have a place.

In her last illness she was attended daily by those faithful subjects who had all along recognized her sovereignty—in Society she was Queen. She surely won her heart's desire, for to that bed from which she was no more to rise, courtiers came and kneeling kissed her hand, and women by the score whom she had befriended paid her the tribute of their tears.

She died in Paris aged fifty-one.

When you are in Switzerland and take the little steamer that plies on Lake Leman from Lausanne to Geneva, you will see on the western shore a tiny village that clings close around a chateau, like little oysters around the parent shell. This is the village of Coppet that you behold, and the central building that seems to be a part of the very landscape is the Chateau De Necker. This was the home of Madame De Stael and the place where so many refugees sought safety.

"Coppet is Hell in motion," said Napoleon. "The woman who lives there has a petticoat full of arrows that could hit a man were he seated on a rainbow. She combines in her active head and strong heart Rousseau and Mirabeau; and then shields herself behind a shift and screams if you approach. To attract attention to herself she calls, 'Help, help!'"

The man who voiced these words was surely fit rival to the chatelaine of this vine-covered place of peace that lies smiling an ironical smile in the sunshine on yonder hillside.

Coppet bristles with history.

Could Coppet speak it must tell of Voltaire and Rousseau, who had knocked at its gates; of John Calvin; of Montmorency; of Hautville (for whom Victor Hugo named a chateau); of Fanny Burney and Madame Recamier and Girardin (pupil of Rousseau); and Lafayette and hosts of others who are to us but names, but who in their day were greatest among all the sons of men.

Chief of all was the great Necker, who himself planned and built the main edifice that his daughter "might ever call it home." Little did he know that it would serve as her prison, and that from here she would have to steal away in disguise. But yet it was the place she called home for full two decades. Here she wrote and wept and laughed and sang: hating the place when here, loving it when away. Here she came when De Stael had died, and here she brought her children. Here she received the caresses of Benjamin Constant, and here she won the love of pale, handsome Rocco, and here, "when past age," gave birth to his child. Here and in Paris, in quick turn, the tragedy and comedy of her life were played; and here she sleeps.

In the tourist season there are many visitors at the chateau. A grave old soldier, wearing on his breast the Cross of the Legion of Honor, meets you at the lodge and conducts you through the halls, the salon and the library. There are many family portraits, and mementos without number, to bring back the past that is gone forever. Inscribed copies of books from Goethe and Schiller and Schlegel and Byron are in the cases, and on the walls are to be seen pictures of Necker, Rocco, De Stael and Albert, the firstborn son, decapitated in a duel by a swinging stroke from a German saber, on account of a king and two aces held in his sleeve.

Beneath the old chateau dances a mountain brook, cold from the Jura; in the great courtway is a fountain and fish-pond, and all around are flowering plants and stately palms. All is quiet and orderly. No children play, no merry voices call, no glad laughter echoes through these courts. Even the birds have ceased to sing.

The quaint chairs in the parlors are pushed back with precision against the wall, and the funereal silence that reigns supreme seems to say that death yesterday came, and an hour ago all the inmates of the gloomy mansion, save the old soldier, followed the hearse afar and have not yet returned.

We are conducted out through the garden, along gravel walks, across the well-trimmed lawn; and before a high iron gate, walled in on both sides with massive masonry, the old soldier stops, and removes his cap. Standing with heads uncovered, we are told that within rests the dust of Madame De Stael, her parents, her children, and her children's children— four generations in all.

The steamer whistles at the wharf as if to bring us back from dream and mold and death, and we hasten away, walking needlessly fast, looking back furtively to see if grim spectral shapes are following after. None is seen, but we do not breathe freely until aboard the steamer and two short whistles are heard, and the order is given to cast off. We push off slowly from the stone pier, and all is safe.

Printed in Great Britain
by Amazon